The Burden & Blessings Of Being Black

The Journey

LORRAINE WATKINS

Watkins Publishing™

Greenville, South Carolina

The Burden & Blessings of Being Black – The Journey

Published by Watkins Publishers™

Greenville, South Carolina

Library of Congress Cataloging in Publication Date, January 6, 2018

ISBN 13: 978-1984927309

Preface

History of Slavery in America Summarized

(1600-1800)

Slavery in America began when the first African slaves were brought to the North American colony of Jamestown, Virginia, in 1619, to aid in the production of such lucrative crops as tobacco. Slavery was practiced throughout the American colonies in the 17th and 18th centuries, and African-American slaves helped build the economic foundations of the new nation. The invention of the cotton gin in 1793 solidified the central importance of slavery to the South's economy. By the mid19th century, America's westward expansion, along with a growing abolition movement in the North, would provoke a great debate over slavery that would tear the nation apart in the bloody American Civil War (1861-65). Though the Union victory freed the nation's 4 million slaves, the legacy of slavery continued to influence American history, from the tumultuous years of Reconstruction (1865-77) to the civil rights movement that emerged in the 1960s, a century after emancipation.

In the early 17th century, European settlers in North America turned to African slaves as a cheaper, more plentiful labor source than indentured servants (who were mostly poorer Europeans). After 1619, when a Dutch ship brought 20 Africans ashore at the British colony of Jamestown, Virginia, slavery spread throughout the American colonies. Though it is impossible to give accurate figures, some historians have estimated that 6 to 7 million slaves were imported to the New World during the 18th century alone, depriving the African continent of some of its healthiest and ablest men and women.

In the 17th and 18th centuries, black slaves worked mainly on the tobacco, rice and indigo plantations of the southern coast. After the American Revolution (1775-83), many colonists (particularly in the North, where slavery was relatively unimportant to the economy) began to link the oppression of black slaves to their own oppression by the British, and to call for slavery's abolition. After the war's end, however, the new U.S. Constitution tacitly acknowledged the institution, counting each slave as three-fifths of a person for the purposes of taxation and representation in Congress and guaranteeing the right to repossess any "person held to service or labor" (an obvious euphemism for slavery).

In the late 18th century, with the land used to grow tobacco nearly exhausted, the South faced an economic crisis, and the continued growth of slavery in America seemed in doubt. Around the same time, the mechanization of the textile industry in England led to a huge demand for American cotton, a southern crop whose production was unfortunately limited by the difficulty of removing the seeds from raw cotton fibers by hand. In 1793, a young Yankee schoolteacher named Eli

Whitney invented the cotton gin, a simple mechanized device that efficiently removed the seeds. His device was widely copied, and within a few years the South would transition from the large-scale production of tobacco to that of cotton, a switch that reinforced the region's dependence on slave labor.

Slavery itself was never widespread in the North, though many of the region's businessmen grew rich on the slave trade and investments in southern plantations. Between 1774 and 1804, all of the northern states abolished slavery, but the so-called "peculiar institution" remained absolutely vital to the South. Though the U.S. Congress outlawed the African slave trade in 1808, the domestic trade flourished, and the slave population in the U.S. nearly tripled over the next 50 years. By 1860 it had reached nearly 4 million, with more than half living in the cotton-producing states of the South.

Slaves in the antebellum South constituted about one-third of the southern population. Most slaves lived on large farms or small plantations; many masters owned less than 50 slaves. Slave owners sought to make their slaves completely dependent on them, and a system of restrictive codes governed life among slaves. They were prohibited from learning to read and write, and their behavior and movement was restricted. Many masters took sexual liberties with slave women, and rewarded obedient slave behavior with favors, while rebellious slaves were brutally punished. A strict hierarchy among slaves (from privileged house slaves and skilled artisans down to lowly field hands) helped keep them divided and less likely to organize against their masters. Slave marriages had no legal basis, but slaves did marry and raise large families; most slave owners encouraged this practice, but nonetheless did not hesitate to divide slave families by sale or removal.

Slave revolts did occur within the system (notably ones led by Gabriel Prosser in Richmond in 1800 and by Denmark Vesey in Charleston in 1822), but few were successful. The slave revolt that most terrified white slaveholders was that led by <u>Nat Turner</u> in Southampton County, Virginia, in August 1831. Turner's group, which eventually numbered around 75 blacks, murdered some 60 whites in two days before armed resistance from local whites and the arrival of state militia forces overwhelmed them. Supporters of slavery pointed to Turner's rebellion as evidence that blacks were inherently inferior barbarians requiring an institution such as slavery to discipline them, and fears of similar insurrections led many southern states to further strengthen their slave codes in order to limit the education, movement and assembly of slaves. In the North, the increased repression of southern blacks would only fan the flames of the growing abolition movement.

From the 1830s to the 1860s, a movement to abolish slavery in America gained strength in the northern United States, led by free blacks such as <u>Frederick Douglass</u> and white supporters such as William Lloyd Garrison, founder of the radical newspaper The Liberator, and <u>Harriet Beecher Stowe</u>, who published the bestselling antislavery novel "Uncle Tom's Cabin" (1852). While many abolitionists based their activism on the belief that slaveholding was a sin, others were more inclined to the non-religious "free-labor" argument, which held that slaveholding was regressive, inefficient and made little economic sense.

Free blacks and other antislavery northerners had begun helping fugitive slaves escape from southern plantations to the North via a loose network of safe houses as early as the 1780s. This practice, known as the <u>Underground Railroad</u>, gained real momentum in the 1830s and although estimates vary widely, it may have helped anywhere from 40,000 to 100,000 slaves reach freedom. The success of the Underground Railroad helped spread abolitionist feelings in the North; it also undoubtedly increased sectional tensions, convincing pro-slavery southerners of their northern countrymen's determination to defeat the institution that sustained them.

America's explosive growth—and its expansion westward in the first half of the 19th century—would provide a larger stage for the growing conflict over slavery in America and its future limitation or expansion. In 1820, a bitter debate over the federal government's right to restrict slavery over Missouri's application for statehood ended in a compromise: <u>Missouri</u> was admitted to the Union as a slave state, <u>Maine</u> as a free state and all western territories north of Missouri's southern border were to be free soil. Although the <u>Missouri Compromise</u> was designed to maintain an even balance between slave and free states, it was able to help quell the forces of sectionalism only temporarily.

In 1850, another tenuous compromise was negotiated to resolve the question of territory won during the Mexican War. Four years later, however, the <u>Kansas-Nebraska</u> Act opened all new territories to slavery by asserting the rule of popular sovereignty over congressional edict, leading pro- and anti-slavery forces to battle it out (with much bloodshed) in the new state of <u>Kansas</u>. Outrage in the North over the Kansas-Nebraska Act spelled the downfall of the old <u>Whig</u>

<u>Party</u> and the birth of a new, all-northern Republican Party. In 1857, the Supreme Court's ruling in the Dred Scott case (involving a slave who sued for his freedom on the grounds that his master had taken him into free territory) effectively repealed the Missouri Compromise by ruling that all territories were open to slavery. The abolitionist John Brown's raid at Harper's Ferry, Virginia, in 1859 aroused sectional tensions even further: Executed for his crimes, Brown

was hailed as a martyred hero by northern abolitionists and a vile murderer in the South.

The South would reach the breaking point the following year, when Republican candidate <u>Abraham Lincoln</u> was elected as president. Within three months, seven southern states had seceded to form the <u>Confederate States of America</u>; four more would follow after the Civil War (1861-65) began. Though Lincoln's antislavery views were well established, the central Union war aim at first was not to abolish slavery, but to preserve the United States as a nation. Abolition became a war aim only later, due to military necessity, growing anti-slavery sentiment in the North and the self-emancipation of many African Americans who fled enslavement as Union troops swept through the South. Five days after the bloody Union victory at Antietam in September 1862, Lincoln issued a preliminary emancipation proclamation, and on January 1, 1863, he made it official that "slaves within any State, or designated part of a State…in rebellion, …shall be then, thenceforward, and forever free."

By freeing some 3 million black slaves in the rebel states, the <u>Emancipation Proclamation</u> deprived the Confederacy of the bulk of its labor forces and put international public opinion strongly on the Union side. Some 186,000 black soldiers would join the Union Army by the time the war ended in 1865, and 38,000 lost their lives. The total number of dead at war's end was 620,000 (out of a population of some 35 million), making it the costliest conflict in American history.

The 13th Amendment, adopted late in 1865, officially abolished slavery, but freed blacks' status in the post-war South remained precarious, and significant challenges awaited during the Reconstruction period (1865-77). Former slaves received the rights of citizenship and the "equal protection" of the Constitution in the 14th Amendment (1868) and the right to vote in the 15th (1870), but the provisions of Constitution were often ignored or violated, and it was difficult for former slaves to gain a foothold in the post-war economy thanks to restrictive black codes and regressive contractual arrangements such as sharecropping.

Despite seeing an unprecedented degree of black participation in American political life, Reconstruction was ultimately frustrating for African Americans, and the rebirth of white supremacy–including the rise of racist organizations such as the Ku Klux Klan–had triumphed in the South by 1877. Almost a century later, resistance to the lingering racism and discrimination in America that began during the slavery era would lead to the civil rights movement of the 1960s, which would achieve the greatest political and social gains for blacks since

Reconstruction.

Lorraine Watkins, Author

Table of Contents

Chapter One

What does it feel like being black?

After you realize that first that your skin color and your culture is different from other cultures around you, then notice that you are looked at differently and treated differently. It almost has a negative connotation to it. It depends on when you were born, in the 18th century, in the 19th century, or in the 21th century because each generation look at the world through similar but different lenses depending on the laws in the country at that time. What did the law say about you during slavery depicts the way you perceive the world's view of you and your view of yourself? However; we need the knowledge of where we come from as a people to where we need to be as the world involve around us. So, feeling good about being black has do with your personal belief about who you are and why you exist or having a positive sense of who you are as a human being will determine how good you feel about yourself. If you were raised in an underprivilege culture and never saw any progress to equality compared to other cultures, you may define yourself as an underclass citizen, but if you were born in a time where you witnessed progress within your culture, you probably could see yourself as a person who can progress and make a difference in the world around you. Regardless of the laws of the land in each segment of the three centuries addressed in this book, 19th, 20th, and 21th century of our world, if you believe that your living or purpose for living or dying is not in vain, then you can survive the times. It's like looking at a pie chart and assessing the slice percentile of the whole pie in sections. As a black people, the pie slice maybe cut very thin in comparison to other cultures when it comes to our health, our economics, our social statue, our privileges, higher education, business industries, home ownership, etc. If you were a share cropper working on someone else's land verses being a share cropper working on your land that you own puts things into a different perspective. If you were born in a time where it was illegal for blacks to vote or to marry outside their race, you may feel less than a man because you are not legally in position to decide how you want to vote because you couldn't vote at all or if you felt in love with a woman or man from a different race at that time when it was illegal to do so, you may have felt like you couldn't love someone who didn't look like you. Even if you were black but looked too white in appearance, you still had a difficult time marrying another black woman if she was darker in skin other than. On the flip side of that coin, it would still be difficult to marry a white woman as well because naturally you were still a black man. There were no rights or privileges for black during slavery and very little at the end of slavery. Blacks had to take what was given to them or work hard with sweat and blood for it. A black woman and former slave was interviewed nationally, who survived slavery noted that she never knew what rest was, and during the interview she was near 95 years old at the time. Imagine living in an era as a slave and not knowing was rest is almost unimaginable today (2018).

The sad thing about that is after all these years, blacks seem to be moving backwards instead of forward in some aspects of the economic ladder in America. Today in America, (2018) millions of blacks are being incarcerated at an alarming rate leaving the mothers to raise their children alone. There you see the breakdown of the family unit again where family are separated whether by reasons of crime committed, or crime invented. Studies and research have shown how we think, feel, and believe in every area of our lives; spiritually, culturally, and literacy. If you were born during slavery, being black was not celebrated like it is today and therefore, being black probably didn't feel good unless you had the knowledge of where you came from in Africa that your life meant something special to your tribal people or ancestors depending on where you came from. You could come from a lineage of royalty and wealth but without that knowledge, you probably wouldn't know where you came from or what your real purpose what in the earth unless you had a spiritual revelation of it. I think that is why black people in general are so spiritual as well as the Indians, they relied on the Spirits to guide them, the stars and the moon and the water and the changing of the seasons to interpret who they were. Blacks depended on food from plants and water for healing, and they depended on each other as much as possible for survival. If you lived in a cold climate or if you lived in a warm climate also influenced your belief system. Most dark-skinned people from Africa were born in warmer climates where the plants grew better vegetation for them to eat food from the earth. There were many animals and fish in the sea. There were huge amounts of gold to sustain the economy and when that is stripped away from you and families separated and enslaved, it makes it difficult to trace back to your ancestors and family. So, you rely on what the slave owners tell you who you are and what you can and cannot do. You are taught a different way of living a new language and a new religion and a new way of feeling about yourself. That's how it was at that time. In order for peace, and to survive, you had to learn how to keep your thoughts and feelings to yourself because it did not matter anyway. Nobody cared what your opinion was about anything during slavery. Animals has more rights than Blacks. A strong nation was broken and brought to their knees by other cultures from all around the world. The main reason was to build their own economy and countries from the backs of blacks from Africa and when the time was expiring to buy male slaves, they then became clever and brought black female slaves so that the reproduction of slaves will keep being populated throughout each region where slaves was being sold to other slave owners and many years went by. Finally, after the civil war in May of 1865, slavery also ended because the North won the war and slavery was emancipated. Blacks was free from slavery but had no money, no land, and nowhere to go so most of them stayed in the South and worked as share croppers. They shared the land and the production of the land. They still had a long way to go to freedom.

Chapter Two

A Grain of Salt

On May 9, 1865, the civil war ended and shortly afterwards so did slavery. A lot of Blacks quickly moved to the North to find jobs and a better life for themselves and their families while others stayed in the South and worked the land as sharecroppers sharing the production of the harvest working for the Whites. Some of the former slave owners sold portions of the land to the Black to crop for themselves. There was a great separation as to what kind of work you were able to do and if you could get an education because reading or learning to read was against the law. How can you compete with others in the world without the same kind of education and knowledge of how the law works, if they could not read nor write? People are destroyed because of the lack of knowledge so there were many barriers to overcome. For a long time, Blacks lived in shacks, houses that wouldn't pass inspection today; holes in the ceiling and holes in the floor. No windows, just had to do the best you could to live in cold winters where many became sick of illnesses and without proper medicine to cure them, they died suddenly. If you were smart however, you learned a trade and earned you a better living for your family. When cotton mills was established, it opened up all kinds of possibilities for not only Blacks but for poor Whites as well. Blacks worked in the plants in the South was large cotton mills where machines would thread the cotton into materials that made clothes and then clothes were sold, and the economy started to flourish among other inventions, etc. We went from horses and buggies to cars. Manufacturing companies that product peanut butter, packing corn, flour, wheat, butter, and lots of other household products and goods. Better ways to manufacturer goods and products made many people rich and famous. Printing and recording the news on the radio was a big advancement for America and laws was being made and passed all the time.

Chapter Three

My Family Economical Story

Let's fast forward to the 1930s. Let me give you a preview of my own family

from North Carolina. When I look through the eye of my parents, Ervin and

Betty Lou Smith Watkins, both born in Stanly County, the city of Albemarle,

North Carolina, and see their facial expressions as they tell me about their

personal lives and the major world events that challenge their strengths and

weaknesses, it made me tremble inside to see how these changes affected

their decisions. Their background and culture consisted o a race of people

called African Americans whose names were culturally changed throughout

history as being called "niggard", "negro", "colored", "black" and today as

"African-Americans" because their major ancestors were born in the African continent. These names are significant and have bearings on the way Blacks were treated throughout history. According to the Merriam-Webster's dictionary, the word Nigger derived earlier from the word Negro; black, dated as far back as to 1786. The meaning of the word is usually offensive relating to a black person or a member of any dark-skinned race.

When my father was born in 1936, the United States Presidential Election took place. This was also during the Great Depression an Franklin Delano Roosevelt was elected president who was a Democrat from New York. He implemented the New Deal program, an economic policy such as Social Security and unemployment benefits. He was the 32nd president of the United States and won by 60.8% of the national popular vote. He provided relief programs such as the Federal Emergency Relief Administration for the unemployed, the Civilian Conservation Corps (CCC) which hired 250,000 unemployed young men to work on rural local projects. Also, during his administration, he broaden the regulation of the Federal Trade Commission to provide mortgage relief to millions if farmers and home owners.

Roosevelt expanded a Hoover agency, the Reconstruction Finance Corporation to help finance the railroads and industry. (us.history.com)

My father was born in 1936 when the Great Depression was entering in its eight year. His father, Mr. Slade Watkins worked as a night guard for the Young Manufacturing Company in Norwood, North Carolina. His mother did domestic work such as cooking and cleaning houses for white women with no more than a 5th grade education and raised four children. His father taught her how to count money and how to read some. His father, Slade Watkins, my grandfather, worked and saved his money and purchased a Ford truck and then brought 8 acres of land and built a big three-bedroom house to raise his four children and take care of this wife, Wilma, my grandmother.

My father was educated in the Stanly County public school system. He was promoted to the tenth but dropped out of high school to marry my mother who was in the ninth grade. She bore six children from this union, four boys and two girls. My father worked as a general laborer, digging ditches, working in the cotton mills, laying bricks, doing carpentry in order to take care of his family. He later became employed by the Wiscasset Mill in Albemarle, North Carolina when these jobs became available to black men. My mother also did domestic work cleaning house and cooking for white families. My father lived in the same house with his father his father built which was originally torn down and rebuilt in the 1950s. There he also farmed for his family, grew his own vegetables, raised chickens, hogs, went fishing and hunting to provide for his family of eight. He brought a brown car from the Chevrolet dealership. My mother's father, Walter Smith, was half Black and half Indian. He worked at

C&A in their cafeteria as a cook. He also worked at hotels and motels as a cook. Her mother, Lona Smith, her step-mother, worked as a domestic worker cleaning and cooking for a white family as well. He purchased a car which was a Plymouth and later brought a house in Porters between Norwood and Albemarle, North Carolina.

He had close to 20 acres of land. He was one of the first black men to purchase a TV, car, and a house in his day. He made his own butter among other things and raised a garden of vegetables, a grape vine, apple trees, and raised hogs as well. My mother spoke of a club that Black women had

in started in their community to save money for Christmas shopping so that

their children would have a good Christmas. My mother mainly cleaned up

their house growing up and her sister Doretha did most of all the cooking

and her brother Herman worked the gardens and did yardwork, later joined

the United States Army and retired as a Lieutenant or General. She had

three other brothers who moved from the South to the North to find better

employment opportunities and earn a higher standard of living of which

they did and purchased their houses and raised their families.

Between years 1939 and 1943, the average new home cost $3,925 to $4,075

and the average income per year was $1,713 to $1,750. A loaf of bread was

12 cents, and to rent a house cost $25 to $32 per month. The price of an

average car was $850. (thepeoplehistory.com)

During this time in 1941, Pearl Harbor was attacked by Japan which

launched the beginning of World War I. The big four allies power o WWII

were the United States of America, England, (Great Britain, the United

Kingdom), the Soviet Union (U.S.S.R.) Russia, and France. (www.worldwar2history.infor/war)

The Japanese air attack on Pearl Harbor was on December 7, 1941. In Pearl Harbor, there were 96 vessels, the bulk of the United States Pacific Fleet. Eight battleships were there, but the air craft carrier was all at sea. The Japanese attacked Pearl Harbor so quickly and left much devastation and casualties. Men were killed and seriously wounded. President Roosevelt was serving a second term and president and he declared war using all the resources of the country. Four days after the attack on Pearl Harbor, Germany and Italy declared war on the United States.

F. D. Roosevelt created the Fair Employment Practices Commission to begin recruiting African Americans Marine in 1942. The Marines first black recruits received basic training at the segregated Mont fort Point Base adjacent to Camp Le jeume, North Carolina and continued to recruit Blacks until 1949.

During WWII, the army was segregated. Black nurses cared mostly for black troops in the states, Africa, England, and Burma. The blood was labeled with an "A:", because African-Americans could not use "white blood and vice versa." Black nurses in World War I, but the Corps did not accept them again until 1941. By the end of the war, only about 500 black women had served in the Corps. (www.guzette.com/articles/nursing)

When black soldiers returned home, they mostly returned to the medial jobs as farmers and laborers. Nothing much had change until the 1960s when blacks fought for equality in jobs, housing, education, and healthcare. There was a standard that everyone was getting equality although it was segregated equality. The black schools did not get the same quality education and used outdated books. The Blacks had to drink from a different water fountain from the Whites and had to sit at the back of the Theatre Movies mainly upstairs.

My parents enjoyed music and the popular songs of B.B. King, Nat King Cole, Little Richard, Lena Horne, the Four Tops, the Temptations, Al Green, Aretha Franklin, to name a few and of course gospel, and Shirley Caesar. When they were dating, they used to love to dance at the local "juke joints" and did dances like "the Twist", "the Mash Potato", and "the Drag."

The popular cigarettes were Campbell and Lucky Stripes. The popular cars manufactured then was Ford, Cadillac, and Chevrolet. The top three brands in products were from Kellogg, Sears, and Macys. The hairs styles for Blacks in the 1950s was slick hair combed back greased with either roe lye or grease with a heart iron hair comb to press out the Afro. Most of the drinking water came from wells or spring water.

The Blacks were not allowed to vote until the Civil Rights Movement (1954-1968) headed by Dr. Martin Luther King Jr. who was a Baptist minister from Alabama and he began protesting and peacefully marching to the White House to stop segregation. He was the spokesman for Blacks everywhere. He gave a voice of hope to the Black people and other minorities who was not treated fairly and whose pay wages were below the whites. He gave speeches to lift the spirits and to give hope to the less fortunate. He had to have been anointed by God to be so brave in trying to create justice for all. In one of his speeches entitled, "I Have a Dream", he states that the dream was about little black girls and little black boys being able to walk together with little white boys and white girls while attending the same schools in peace and harmony.

It was a powerful speech and is repeated every year until this day during Black History Month in February. There was a woman by the name of Rosa Parks who then 42 years old, refused to give up seat on the public bus to a white person simply because she was very tired from working all day, was arrested and jailed because it was against the law for Blacks to sit at the front of the bus. This began boycotts and sit-ins against segregation on buses and against not be able to sit and eat in restaurants where the whites where sitting and eating.

Black refused to ride the bus and rather walked to work or to school. They were not allowed to vote in campaign elections and many were beaten, jailed, and even killed to earn the same rights as whites did. Blacks wanted equality across the board, equal jobs and equal pay, equal housing, healthcare, education and the rights to purchased and own land and property like the whites. They paid a grave price for these rights. When it's time to vote, we must exercise our legal right to vote. We should exercise our rights to be enrolled in the best colleges to get the best education.

It is our responsibility to educate our children socially, politically, economically, and legally on their rights and privileges. For it takes a village to raise our children. We must prepare them how to be self-suffient and how to be independent in creating wealth for themselves in this new era of life.

Summary

We go to church to keep our spirits lifted and encouraged. The holy bible tells us to love our enemies and pray for them who despitefully. As time has progress toward the 21st century, we have witnessed many changes in our economy and women have proven to be just as efficient as men in the work force holding down working outside the home and raising a family. Women have not only become school teachers, school principals educating our children, they are business owners, home owners, they are driving 18 wheelers, police officers, enforcing the law. They are in the court room not only as attorneys but also as judges. They are also standing tall in the arena or politics, passing legislations, and running for the congressional seast in the White House. We have witness having a black man as the president of the United States of America as former President Barack Obama in (2008 – 2016) serving two terms and having a classy leading first lady, Michelle Robinson Obama by his side who hold a degree in Law. We are business owners, air pilots, ministers, recording artists, film producers, talk show hosts, book authors. We have the opportunity of a life time at our finger tips. Let's continue to move forward by the grace of God. We need to remember how far we have come as a people.

The burden of being black is feeling the need to constantly prove yourself to others how you measure up; whether its maintaining a business, investing money, to raising your family, or simply being enough. I think we consciously and unconsciously feel the need to be accepted by other cultures or to need the feeling of belonging to a group whether it's in our own community or the community of others to a certain degree. When we embrace our own culture of people more and have an appreciation for who we are as a people, we can embrace others all in the name of humanity, love, and respect for the way other societies live out their culture differences. I remember back in the 1970s feeling a strong sense of black pride in our community and across America. We had a stronger tide of sisterhood, brotherhood, and community-hood. As we approached the 1980s, and as more women were becoming more of their own power-house in business, education, and managing their lives independent of a man, the community started advancing economically, but the family units were beginning to unthread. Black churches were very strong in their faith and engaging in upgrading and building their communities. Also, it was then a break out in the AIDS academic, and a stronger rise in drug use that really brought the walls down in the black urban communities. When family suffers, the community suffer, and it is a known fact across the board. The fact is that how we respond to the world and how the world response to us begins with the way we are raised as a child.

It is important that we vote for the people whether black or white, republican or demonstrate to help us achieve our agenda. These are the people who legislate laws, make and create laws that we all live by, they create policies every day that will affect all our lives. As you progress in your businesses and careers, never forget to reach back and help your brothers and sisters who are striving to reach the same measure of success.

Know your rights when it comes to fair housing, fair labor, economics growth in our communities, and together we can change this world around. It doesn't have to end up another sad song and another sad story. Strong families' equal strong communities. Let's stick together and help make this world a better place to live in one community as a time. There will always be obstacles, and mountains to climb, but if we believe in a united America, we can achieve our dreams not blame others for our failures and inaccuracies. We have come such a long way in our society through war times, and the ups and downs of our economy, and we survived before and we can do it again today. We have to understand where we have been in history to understand where we need to go. In hopes of one peaceful nation under God with liberty, and justice for all people. We now live in a multi-cultured society and with that in mind, we must respect another's beliefs, values, and faith. We must strive to live in harmony side by side whether in peace time or in war time. We must stand all as an American and be proud of the great men who have led the way to our victories and learn from our failures. Together we can achieve great things, we are better together. We are stronger together.

Keep your eyes on the prize of the higher calling and purpose in life. Keep the faith and stay strong. Do not be hypnotized into thinking that you cannot, because yes you can bring about a change in your family, your community, and your country. Rise up, stand up and lets move forward to strengthen the next generation and the generations to come.

About the Author

Lorraine Watkins is a 17 time author and a graduate of Gardner-Webb University of North Carolina. She has been an ordained minister of the gospel of Jesus Christ since year 2000. Lorraine is currently residing in the beautiful city of Greenville, South Carolina and is an active member and associate minister of the Mount Pleasant Missionary Baptist Church, Greenville, South Carolina where Dr. Joseph Howard III is the pastor. She has one daughter, Jacqueline Berghauser, RN, and one grandson, Marcario Isaiah Parks, 11th grader attending J. L. Mann High School. She is also the author of "Ways to Manage Anxiety", a self-help manual. As an native of Stanly County, North Carolina, she volunteered in her community as an Substitute Teacher grade K-12th, office administrator, and worked in many compacities in ministry. She is called upon to speak to women groups and conferences on how to achieve your dreams, combating adversity through the power of prayer. To book a workshop with Lorraine Watkins, contact her direct at 1+704-438-2815 and leave a detailed message.

www.ingramcontent.com/pod-product-compliance
Lightning Source LLC
Chambersburg PA
CBHW040201240726
48664CB00002B/784